*Watch for these additional holiday books
written by the same author:*
**THE PUMPKIN BOOK
THE THANKSGIVING BOOK
THE BUNNY BOOK**

Published by
PUMPKIN PRESS PUBLISHING HOUSE™
P.O. Box 139, Shasta, CA 96087

THE ELVES' CHRISTMAS BOOK

FULL OF THE SEASON'S HISTORY, POEMS, SONGS, ART PROJECTS, GAMES AND RECIPES

For Parents and Teachers to use with young Children.

Written and Illustrated by
SUSAN OLSON HIGGINS

Written and published by Susan Olson Higgins

PUMPKIN PRESS

P.O. Box 139
Shasta, CA 96087

Dedicated to all those musty, dusty trips down the chimney Santa made for me . . .

. . . and to my dear-to-my heart brother and sister, Philip and Linda, who share memories, adventures and delights of Christmases past.

(Remember feeding the bobbing red cardnals on the snowy Norwood window sill? . . . and the J.H.S. Christmas concerts? . . . and the church pageants? . . . and finding the gifts hiding on the top shelf of the closet?)

It was *wonderful sharing it all with you!*
I LOVE you!

A NOTE TO THE EDITOR:

Thank you V.I. Wexner for orchestrating these pages into superb harmony.

PREFACE

'Tis a season full of merriment, love, joy, and giving. Tuck a little of this Christmas spirit into your stocking. Pull it out from time to time throughout the coming year and share it with your fellow man.

God bless you everyone.

Susan Olson Higgins

TABLE OF CONTENTS

HERE IS A HINT: READ ALL OF THE
DIRECTIONS BEFORE YOU BEGIN A PROJECT.

THE HISTORY OF CHRISTMAS
by Gail C. Nall

"Silent Night! Holy Night!" "Glory to the Newborn King," "Peace on Earth," "O Come Let us Adore Him" are melodies which have gloriously echoed in harmony throughout the Earth in celebration of Christmas. It all began in a small stable in Bethlehem with the birth of the Christ Child. The wonder and joyousness of the night has inspired people from around the world to sing forth with jubilation these same songs for hundreds of years. Even Shakespeare spoke of the glory of the night of Christ's birth, "so hallow'd and so gracious is the time." *(Hamlet)*

The word "Christmas" originated from an early English phrase, "Cristes Masse," meaning mass of Christ. The date, December 25, was established in 354 A.D. by Bishop Liberius of Rome when he selected it as the official time for celebrating Christ's birth. Until this time the birth of Jesus was observed on many different days. Even now no one is sure of the exact date of His birth.

The celebration of Christmas has come to mean many different things to different people. Traditions have developed and been passed on from generation to generation until there exists a tremendous wealth of customs surrounding the holiday. The joy of Christmas comes wrapped in shining lights, jolly Santas, carol singing, cookies baking, kisses under mistletoe, glimmering trees, the warmth of family, brightly colored packages ... and the true Spirit of Christmas has never changed; but rather spreads through out the world through our giving.

THE CHRISTMAS TREE

It is believed the Christmas tree custom originated in Germany. In medieval times, it was common practice to welcome guests by lighting candles on a tree. Eventually, the delightful practice evolved into a Christmas tradition.

The Christmas tree was brought to America by German immigrants. The custom quickly spread and became an annual ritual in homes across the country.

The Christmas tree was introduced in England a little over 100 years ago when Queen Victoria married German Prince Albert. Wherever Christmas trees stand, you can be sure they light joy in the hearts of those who catch even a glimpse of their glimmering beauty.

SENDING CHRISTMAS CARDS

This tradition began in London, England when beautiful greetings were scrolled on cards with lavish designs of flowers, birds, etc. The first cards were sent around 1850. Slowly their popularity grew until they have become one of the most delightful customs of the season, bringing old friends and family close to heart at Christmas time.

SAINT NICHOLAS - SANTA CLAUS

Saint Nicholas was born in the third century. He dedicated his entire life to helping mankind . . . especially children. On December 6, he died, but the love and recollection of his great deeds, especially for children, lived on. And so, in many countries December 6 became Saint Nicholas' Day . . . when gifts were given to children.

Santa Claus was "born" in the United States when Clement Moore wrote his famous poem, "The Night Before Christmas" one Christmas eve in New York. He transformed the saintly, charitable character in long robes into a plump, rosy cheeked and jolly old man in a red suit with a team of reindeer and a sleigh.

Of course, Saint Nicholas has many names in many lands, such as Father Christmas in England, Le Pere Noel in France, Kriss Kringle in Germany, and San Nicolass in the Netherlands. And he arrives at different times on different dates, but everywhere he delivers gifts and the spirit of love and joy to children. That is universal.

THE CHRISTMAS STOCKING

Legend has it that long ago, Santa flew over house tops and chimneys in a sleigh being pulled by reindeer. As he passed one chimney, he dropped some coins down, intending them to land on the hearth. Instead, the coins landed in some stockings hanging by the warm fire to dry. So, from then on, stockings were hung by the chimney with care in hopes that Santa would fill them to the brim.

In some countries, wooden shoes are placed on the hearth instead of stockings. In others, Santa leaves a switch or a piece of black coal for bad girls and boys, and treats for the good. However it all began, I am not going to forget to hang MY stocking this Christmas are you?

MERRY CHRISTMAS IN OTHER LANGUAGES

Swedish	God Jul!
German	Froehliche Weinachten!
English	Merry Christmas!
Spanish	Felices Navidad!
Italian	Bon Natale!
French	Joyeux Noel!
Danish	Glaedelig Jul!
Portuguese	Boas Festas!
Finnish	Hauskaa Joulaua!
Brazilian	Boas Festas! or Feliz Natal!

CAROL-SINGING

The word "carol" originally meant a circle dance accompanied by a song. The first caroling was practiced by the Waits in the fourteenth century. Waits were royal singers who were sent by the court to perform in selected homes for pennies and treats, or for fun.

Many of the Christmas carols we hear today were composed between the 1400 and 1600's. The tradition of the Waits was carried on at Christmas time, with groups of people joyfully singing Christmas songs door to door. It was Washington Irving who dubbed this tradition "carol-singing." And, of course, the practice continues today. So spread a little harmony and Christmas cheer this season. Join together with your friends and neighbors in the carol-singing tradition and give the gift of joy.

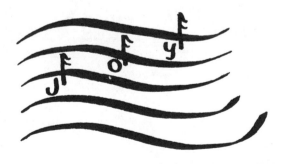

CHANUKAH *(or Hannukah)*

Chanukah is an eight-day celebration beginning each year on the 25th day of the Hebrew month of Kislev. It is a time set aside to honor the defeat of the Syrian army and the re-dedication of the Temple of Jerusalem.

More than 2000 years ago, a Syrian king named Antiochus Epiphanes became very angry when the Jews refused to obey him and follow his laws. He ordered the Jews to stop practicing their religion and he placed pagan alters in the Jewish temple.

The Jews organized their own army led by Judah Maccabee. His army drove the Syrians out of Israel after three long years of fighting. Filled with triumph and joy, the Jews cleaned their Temple, removing the unclean animals and idols left by the Syrians.

They searched for some oil to re-light their *menorah*, the eight-branched candelabrum that was to light the temple at all times. They could find only one small jar of oil that would burn for one day. But a miracle occured. The light continued to burn for eight full days instead of one. Chanukah commemorates this miracle.

Today, Chanukah is celebrated by lighting the candles of the menorah for eight days, one the first day, two the second, etc. Children often play a game with a spinning top called a *dreidle*. A special holiday food is served called *latkes*, or potato pancakes.

ELFISH POEMS

BUSY ELVES

by Susan Olson Higgins

One little elf sat on Santa's knee.
Two little elves trimmed the Christmas tree.
Three little elves shined the reindeer hoofs.
Four little elves counted children's roofs.
Five little elves painted all the trains.
Six little elves wrapped candy canes.
Seven little elves bounced Christmas balls.
Eight little elves dressed pretty dolls.
Nine little elves put toys in the sleigh,
All getting ready for Christmas day.

PEEKING

by Susan Olson Higgins

There are his toes!
There's his foot! There's an ankle
Full of soot! Ick!

There's his leg!
I see his knee! This is it!
He's visiting me!

I see his waist!
And big black belt. I hope that Santa
Doesn't melt!

There's his arm!
What's in his hand? I think this year
Will be just grand.

There's a shoulder!
Look! His head! I'm so glad
I'm not in bed!

What's he doing?
I can't see. He's over by
The Christmas tree.

He's near the stockings
Where they're hung. He is turning . . .
Oh . . . he must be done.

Back to the chimney
Up he goes. He disappeared
From head to toes.

Now I know.
You see, it's true . . . Santa's as real
As me and you.

DOES SANTA WEAR STOCKINGS?

by Peter Michael Olson Higgins

The stockings were hung by the chimney.
"I wonder," the little one said,
"If Santa will fill them with presents,
Or put them on instead."

THE ELF CLOWN *(action poem)*

by Susan Olson Higgins

*As you read this poem, have the children
follow the directions they hear.*

Stand in circle,
Hold hands tight,
Begin to walk
To the right. *(Pause while they walk)*

Now everybody
Spin around;
Slap your knees,
Then touch the ground.

Jump up tall,
Tap your toe;
Tap it fast,
Tap it slow.

Snap your fingers,
Reach up high;
Clap your hands,
Up in the sky.

All you elves,
Sit right down.
Choose someone
To be Elf Clown.

*(At this time, choose someone to be the Elf Clown who will lead the
class in a game of "Follow the Leader." After a minute or two,
choose another Elf Clown to be leader.)*

MY RIDE WITH SANTA

by Susan Olson Higgins

Over the tree tops
Above the roof
I am going to help Santa steer!

Between the mountains
Under the bridge
Whoops! Am I too near?

Around the corner
Into a cloud
Fly fast, you fleet-footed deer!

Under the moon
Around a star
Listen! Can you hear?

Beneath the bells
Past the brook.
The night is cold and clear.

Back down the chimney
And into bed.
Can I help again next year?

*(This could be used as an action poem. Have the children draw
and cut out whatever the sleigh flies past. Tape pictures around
the room, then have the children follow the directions of the poem.)*

SANTA'S SPIES

by Susan Olson Higgins

I just saw him!
Didn't you?
One of Santa's elves
Just peeked through!

He pressed his nose
On the window pane.
His hat was covered
With candy cane.

I think he's here
To see if I'm good
And doing all
The things I should.

I'm sure I saw him
Peeking in right there!
I think I'll be good now . . .
"Would you like to share?"

WAITING FOR CHRISTMAS

by Susan Olson Higgins

When will be Christmas EVER be here?
I think I am going to explode!
Do you think Santa packed enough?
Can the reindeer carry the load?

When will Christmas E V E R be here?
I can **hardly** wait!
I try to be patient . . . but I can't!
Why is Christmas so late?

When will Christmas E V E R be here?
The days go by soooo s l o w.
I've been waiting and waiting so long.

OH! Now Where did Christmas go?

WHERE IS SANTA IN THE SPRING?

by Peter Michael Olson Higgins

Where is Santa in the Spring?
Underneath the trees!
Where his snoring is a roaring . . .
Do not wake him, please!

MY KITTEN AT CHRISTMAS

My kitten at Christmas
Hides tucked under me.
She watches with wonder
Our grand Christmas tree.

The Christmas balls shining
All colored so bright,
The tinsel strings dancing
And sparkling with light,

The tiny glass angels
Whose wings seem to fly,
The brave Christmas clown
Waves as kitten walks by.

The candy canes hanging
Say, "Come take a lick
Of my red and white striped
peppermint stick."

My small fluffy kitten
Sits looking in awe.
Then slowly and carefully,
Lifts up her paw.

She reaches so quickly
To catch some delight,
Those friends in the tree
Shiver with fright!

The bells ring a warning,
The lights wink and blink.
The Santas all bob asking,
"What do you think?"

Because of the flurry,
The tree bends to say,
"Oh, kitten, it's Christmas,
Please do stay away!"

So I gather my kitten
Up on my lap,
Where she purrs through Christmas
. . and then takes a nap.

By Susan
Olson Higgins

18

SNOWBALL ATTACK

by Susan Olson Higgins

Z-z-z-z-z--zip
Wing-g-g
Splop, kerplee-e-e-e!
He got my knee!

Sz-z-z-z-z-z-z-z
Plop
Zing-g-g-g-g-g
That had a sting!

Kerplunk
Splot
Splat
Enough of that!

Sh-h-h-h-h-h
Foooooosh
Zoom
He's met his doom.

F-f-f-f-t-t
Swooooosh
Smack!
I got him back!

(You might wish to discuss snowball-throwing safety after reading this poem, then try the activity on page 53 of this book.)

A CHRISTMAS RIDDLE

by Joshua Daniel Olson Higgins

It loves to nibble sugar lumps.
It never lands with knocks or bumps.
It has tall antlers on its head.
It's usually found around a sled.
What is it? *(Santa's reindeer!)*

SANTA'S ACTION POEM

by Susan Olson Higgins

Blink, blink,
Turn around,
Santa's on his way!

Jump, Jump
Clap your hands,
Hop into his sleigh.

Down, up,
Up, down,
Bending o so slow.

Cross your arms,
Touch your head,

Up the chimney you go!

ELVES ANSWER CLAPPING
(action poem)

by Susan Olson Higgins

Come and clap this poem with me.
Clap your hands or tap your knee.
Tap two for yes and three for no,
Clap the answer as we go.

Let's begin . . .

Santa Claus is a big mouse. *(clap, clap, clap)*
Elves live in a mushroom house. *(clap, clap, clap)*

Christmas trees are always blue. *(clap, clap, clap)*
I can jump a mountain, can you? *(clap, clap, clap)*

Santa Claus is dressed in red. *(clap, clap, sh-h)*
He won't come 'til you're in bed. *(clap, clap, sh-h)*

Reindeer pull old Santa's sleigh. *(clap, clap, sh-h)*
He leaves toys for Christmas day. *(clap, clap, sh-h)*

Santa Claus has two green ears. *(clap, clap, clap)*
He's been asleep for years and years. *(clap, clap, clap)*

Santa Claus walks on his hands. *(clap, clap, clap)*
He grows taller whenever he stands. *(clap, clap, clap)*

Santa's sleigh flies underground. *(clap, clap, clap)*
Reindeer make a roaring sound. *(clap, clap, clap)*

Now my silly poem is through. *(clap, clap, sh-h)*
Write more verses, please, will you? *(clap, clap, sh-h)*

CHRISTMAS DELIGHTS

by Susan Olson Higgins

All the twinkling,
Dancing, winking,
Bright and blinking
Lights.
Bouncing, playing,
As they're saying:

Come join us
Tonight.

A CHRISTMAS RIDDLE

by Dan Higgins

What is red and white and red and white and
red and white?

Answer: A candy cane rolling down a hill.

THE MAGICAL TRIP

by Susan Olson Higgins

(Before you begin reading this poem, put on "The Nutcracker Suite" by Tchaikovsky)

The reindeer leaped over laughing brook;
They wanted to take another look
To see if Santa was ready to go
Over candy mountains and ice cream snow.

Santa nodded. It was time
To take their magical Christmas climb.
So up over rooftops they did glide
Finally taking their Christmas ride.

They stopped upon each chocolate house
Greeted by a sugar plum mouse,
While Santa delivered each magical toy
To every gingerbread girl and boy.

Then up and over the silvery trees
Past sleepy bears and bumble bees,
They sailed on 'till twilight came
And then they flew back home again.

MERRY DAYS!

by Susan Olson Higgins

Christmas candy fills the jars
Trees are decked with radiant stars.

Long red stockings carefully hung
Grand old carols happily sung.

Snowflakes waltz upon the breeze
Snowmen excuse an occasional sneeze.

Presents piled upon the floor
Children peek behind each door.

The wreath is hung. The fire's ablaze.
Cookies adorned with sugary glaze.

Christmas music fills the air
Singing to hearts everywhere,

And all the people on the street
Extend a smile to those they meet.

Yes, the season has begun.
Merry Christmas, everyone!

WHAT ELVES SING

We wish you a merry Christmas,
We wish you a merry Christmas,
We wish you a merry Christmas,
And a happy New Year!

DECK THE HALLS

Old Welsh Tune

Deck the halls with boughs of holly,
Fa la la la la la la la la,
'Tis the season to be jolly,
Fa la la la la la la la la,
Don we now our gay apparel,
Fa la la la la la la la la,
Troll the ancient yule-tide carol,
Fa la la la la la la la la,

See the blazing yule before us,
Fa la la la la la la la la,
Strike the harp and join the chorus,
Fa la la la la la la la la,
Follow me in merry measure,
Fa la la la la la la la la,
While I tell of yule-tide treasure,
Fa la la la la la la la la.

CRADLE HYMN

Martin Luther   J.E. Spilman
(written for children)

Away in a manger, no crib for his bed,
The little Lord Jesus lay down His sweet head;
The stars in the sky looked down where He lay,
The little Lord Jesus asleep in the hay.

The cattle are lowing, the poor baby wakes.
But little Lord Jesus no crying He makes;
I love Thee, Lord Jesus, look down from the sky,
And stay by my cradle till morning is nigh.

SILENT NIGHT

Franz Gruber

Teach your children to sign this immortal Christmas carol. The signs are pictured above each word.

Silent   night!   Holy   Night!

All   is   calm,   All   is   bright.

Round   yon Virgin   Mother and   Child!

Holy   Infant, so   tender and   mild.

Sleep   in   Heavenly   peace.

Sleep   in   Heavenly   peace.

JINGLE BELLS

by J.S. Pierpont

Dashing through the snow,
In a one horse open sleigh,
Over the fields we go,
Laughing all the way.

Bells on bob-tails ring
Making spirits bright,
Oh what fun to ride and sing
A sleighing song tonight.

Chorus:
Oh, jingle bells, jingle bells,
Jingle all the way
Oh what fun it is to ride
In a one horse open sleigh!

Oh, jingle bells, jingle bells,
Jingle all the way.
Oh what fun it is to ride
In a one horse open sleigh!

Chorus in Spanish;

Casca beles, casca beles,
Suenan por todas partes.
O que gusto es el dar
Paseo or trineo.

Casca beles, casca beles,
Suenan por todas partes.
O que gusto es el dar
Paseo por trineo.

TWELVE DAYS OF CHRISTMAS

English   1760

On the first day of Christmas
My true love gave to me
A partridge in a pear tree.

On the second day of Christmas
My true love gave to me
Two turtle doves,
And a partridge in a pear tree.

On the third day of Christmas
My true love gave to me
Three French hens, two turtle doves,
And a partridge in a pear tree.

On the fourth day of Christmas
My true love gave to me
Four calling birds,
Three French hens, two turtle doves,
And a partridge in a pear tree.

On the fifth day of Christmas
My true love gave to me
Five golden rings! Four calling birds,
Three French hens, two turtle doves,
And a partridge in a pear tree.

On the sixth day of Christmas
My true love gave to me,
Six geese a-laying
Five golden rings! Four calling birds,
Three French hens, two turtle doves,
And a partridge in a pear tree.

On the seventh day...Seven swans a-swimming.
On the eighth day...Eight maids a-milking.
On the ninth day...Nine ladies dancing.
On the tenth day...Ten lords a-leaping.
On the eleventh day...Eleven pipers piping.
On the twelfth day...Twelve drummers drumming.

UP ON THE HOUSETOP

Traditional

Up on the housetop reindeer pause,
Out jumps good old Santa Claus;
Down through the chimmey with lots of toys,
All for the little ones, Christmas joys.

Ho, ho, ho! Who wouldn't go!
Ho, ho, ho! Who wouldn't go!
Up on the housetop, click, click, click,
Down through the chimney with good Saint Nick.

First comes the stocking of little Nell;
Oh dear Santa, fill it well;
Give her a dolly that laughs and cries,
One that can open and shut its eyes.

(Refrain)

Look in the stocking of little Will;
Oh, just see what a glorious fill!
Here is a hammer and lots of tacks,
Whistle and ball and a whip that cracks.

(Refrain)

ELFEN ART FUN

ELF DOLL

MATERIALS YOU WILL NEED
approximately 8x12" of green cotton material
two pre-cut red felt triangles
needle
thread
scissors
an adult to supervise the sewing
polyester stuffing

WHAT TO DO
1. Cut the elf doll into the shape shown at the right.
2. Put wrong sides together and stitch along outside of the doll all the way around with an overcast stitch. Leave a small opening along one leg to stuff the doll.
3. Stuff the doll with the polyester stuffing.
4. Close the opening where you stuffed the doll by stitching it the rest of the way.
5. Draw a face on the doll with a magic marker.
6. Stitch the two felt triangles together to make a hat for the elf.
7. Take dictation as the child tells a story about the adventures of the elf.

HINT: Make sure the thread is not too long for the child's arm to pull through the stitch.

SANTA'S SLEIGH ON DISPLAY

MATERIALS YOU WILL NEED
   one small table, approximately 2x3 ft.
   red butcher or wrapping paper
   white cotton or stuffing for pillows
   scissors
   masking tape
   glue
   small chair

WHAT TO DO
1. Turn the table upside down.
2. Wrap the red paper around the outside of the table legs. Secure the paper to the legs with tape.
3. Glue a thin line of cotton or batting around the top of the sleigh.
4. Set the small chair inside the sleigh for Santa's seat.
5. Allow the children to carefully climb aboard Santa's sleigh for a ride!

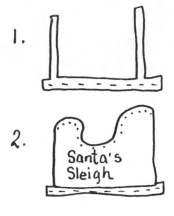

POEM, PEN AND SONG

MATERIALS YOU WILL NEED

crayons, magic marker
paper
Tchaikovsky's "Nutcracker Suite" on tape or
record
poem, "The Magical Trip," on page 23 of this
book. *(Note: any happy holiday poem
and musical arrangement will do!)*

WHAT TO DO

1. Begin playing "The Nutcracker Suite" for the
children.
2. Read "The Magical Trip."
3. Ask the children to illustrate Santa's magical
trip while they listen to the music. Read the
poem once more for the children.
4. Ask them to tell you about their picture when it
is through. Write what they dictate on the page.
5. Ask the children where they would journey if
they could take a ride with Santa.

STITCH A STOCKING

MATERIALS YOU WILL NEED

two 12x18" sheets construction paper
hole puncher
yarn
tempera paint and brush

WHAT TO DO

1. Cut the two sheets of construction paper into
the shape of a stocking.
2. Paint holiday designs on the stocking. Set
aside to dry.
3. Punch holes around the edge of stocking for
stitching.
4. With the yarn, stitch the front to the back
stocking. Tie a loop at the end to hang it.

PAINT A CHRISTMAS ROCK

MATERIALS YOU WILL NEED
    one flat rock
    one or more colors of enamel paint
    one or more fine paint brushes or tooth picks
    newspaper

WHAT TO DO
1. Decide on a simple subject to paint before beginning.
2. Set your materials on newspaper.
3. With paint brush or toothpicks, paint your rock.
4. Set aside to dry.
5. Use it as a paper weight.

FELT CHRISTMAS BANNER

MATERIALS YOU WILL NEED
    one 8x12" felt piece
    multi-colored felt scraps, various
      sizes
    tacky glue
    sewing scissors
    one 12" dowel rod or branch
    two 1x3" felt tabs

WHAT TO DO
Hint: Do not begin until you have decided what you will create.
1. From felt scraps, cut out the design and lay it out on the 8x12" felt piece.
2. Glue each piece where it is placed.
3. Glue the tabs to the top. Set aside to dry.
4. Run the dowel rod or branch through the tabs then display this colorful holiday banner.

CHRISTMAS NAPKIN RINGS

MATERIALS YOU WILL NEED
  Christmas paper, felt, or cloth
  ribbon, yarn, dried flowers or holly
  white glue or tacky glue
  scissors
  cardboard paper towel core or short lengths of
    PVC pipe

WHAT TO DO
1. Cut the cardboard paper core or PVC pipe into 2 inch sections. Those will be your napkin rings.
2. Cover each ring with either cloth, felt, or Christmas paper.
3. Decorate the rings by gluing on holly, dried flowers, ribbon, or yarn.
4. Wrap them and give them as early Christmas gifts to be used for Christmas morning breakfast.

VARIATION: Teach tieing knots or bows while making a napkin ring with thin rope, or silver string.

FELT CHRISTMAS TREE

MATERIALS YOU WILL NEED
one 3x3" green felt square
3" coffee filters
scissors

WHAT TO DO
1. Cut a Christmas tree from the felt.
2. Display the felt tree on a wall or bulletin board.
3. Fold and cut the coffee filters into snowflakes.
4. Hang the coffee filter snowflakes on the tree.

VARIATION: Cut tiny felt ornaments and glue on felt details. Put them on the tree.

STITCH A GIFT

MATERIALS YOU WILL NEED
one 3" diameter embroidery hoop
one 5x5" square of material (no patterns, please)
embroidery thread
needle
an adult to supervise sewing
scissors

WHAT TO DO
1. Secure the material in the embroidery hoop.
3. Draw a SIMPLE design in the center of the material (tree, heart, LOVE, JOY, MOM, bird, flower, etc.)
3. Stitch over the penciled design.
4. Glue the ribbon around the edge of the hoop. Tie a bow at the top. Wrap it for a lovely gift.

   NOTE: Have the needles threaded and knotted, ready to go ahead of time.

MARY BURNS' MACARONI ORNAMENT

MATERIALS YOU WILL NEED
   paper plates
   scissors
   hole puncher
   glue
   macaroni
   gold spray paint
   red yarn
   newspaper

WHAT TO DO
   1. Lay newspaper flat on working surface.
   2. Cut two 3" circles, stars, bells, wreaths, or other holiday shapes.
   3. Punch a hole at the top of each circle so they line up.
   4. Glue macaroni noodles onto both circles.
   5. Set aside to dry.
   6. On the newspaper, spray paint both sides of the ornament gold.
   7. Allow them to dry.
   8. Glue the front and back together.
   9. Tie a red yarn loop through the holes, then hang this golden ornament on the tree.

CLOTH CHRISTMAS BELL

MATERIALS YOU WILL NEED

two 12x18" pre-cut bell-shaped pieces of muslin

material markers, or tempera paint

paint brush

scissors

materials scraps or yarn pre-cut to the width of the bell

material glue or tacky glue

one pre-cut felt circular clacker

stuffing material

WHAT TO DO

1. Decorate both pieces of the muslin bell with material markers, tempera paint, or material scraps and glue.
2. Putting wrong sides together, stuff and glue the bell in three sections, top, middle and bottom by following steps 3, 4 and 5.
3. First, lay stuffing on the upper 1/3 of bell. Lay a small loop of yarn at the top for a hanger. Now glue all around the edges of the stuffing in this upper portion.
4. Lay stuffing in the middle section of the bell and glue the edges.
5. Lay stuffing in the bottom section of the bell, plus yarn attached to felt clacker. Glue the edges.
6. Hang the bell in the window. Write a story about "When Santa rings this bell . . ."

VARIATION: Paint a Christmas bell. Use the child's hand print as the clacker.

PLASTER FOOT PRINT

MATERIALS YOU WILL NEED
    container of moist, soft sand
    pre-mixed, prepared plaster of paris
    newspaper
    tempera paint and brush (optional)
    one small sprig of a dried flower

WHAT TO DO
1. Carefully press bare foot into moist, wet sand.
2. Lift foot without disturbing the impression.
3. Pour the liquid plaster of paris into the foot print in the sand. Push a sprig of a dried flower between the first two toes. Let it stand about one hour or until it has hardened.
4. Carefully brush away the excess sand.
5. When it is thoroughly dry, paint with tempera if you wish, or leave the footprint "natural."

HOLIDAY DISH TOWEL

MATERIALS YOU WILL NEED
    fabric markers
    plain muslin dish towel

WHAT TO DO
1. Draw a holiday design (hearts, a name, "I love you", or patterns) on one end of the dish towel.
2. This gift will be a keepsake!

VARIATION: Draw on a white bib apron for another personal gift idea.

MARYJO'S SANTA IN THE CHIMNEY

MATERIALS YOU WILL NEED

one milk carton
one strip red construction paper to cover milk carton
one cotton ball
black felt tip pen
white glue
scissors

WHAT TO DO

1. Open the top of the milk carton. Cut off the bottom.
2. Cover the carton with red paper. Glue it on to the container. The chimney for Santa is ready!
3. Draw eyes, nose and mouth on one end of the tongue depressor.
4. Cut a tiny slit at the top of the triangle piece of material. Slip it over the top of the tongue depressor for Santa's hat.
5. Wrap the two triangle corners around Santa's "belly" of the tongue depressor. Glue the ends together to make his suit of clothes.
6. Glue the white cotton on Santa's chin for a beard. Glue a tiny bit of cotton to the top and brim of his hat.
7. Place Santa in the chimney. Read the poem on page 12 called "PEEKING", while the children slide their Santa up and down the chimney.

JACQUE GRUBB'S CLAY POCKET

MATERIALS YOU WILL NEED
self-drying or oven-bake clay
waxed paper
rolling pin
nail
dull knife
tiny dry flowers

WHAT TO DO
1. Roll the clay to about ½" thickness on the waxed paper.
2. Cut a 4x9" rectangle.
3. Fold the bottom edge up towards the center to make a pocket.
4. Put two fingers inside the "pocket" and press the edges together against the bottom. Use a dab of water if needed to join the edges.
5. Using the point of the nail, draw designs in the clay on the pocket and above it.
6. Using the nail, poke a hole near the top to hang it.
7. Set aside to dry. Add the dry flowers in the pocket, then hang it on the wall. This makes a lovely gift.

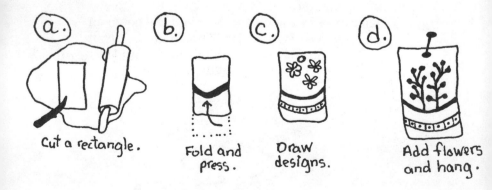

a. Cut a rectangle.

b. Fold and press.

c. Draw designs.

d. Add flowers and hang.

FROSTY THE SNOWMAN

MATERIALS YOU WILL NEED

    2x6" strips of white construction paper
    paste or white glue
    one black 12x18" sheet construction paper
    one small orange paper triangle
    one red paper smile
    2 foot high snowman cut from butcher paper

WHAT TO DO

1. Roll the first 2x6" strip into a ring. Glue the ends together.
2. Pass the next strip through the center of the first ring, then glue the ends together. Continue until you have a chain.
3. When the chain is complete, begin gluing it onto the snowman. Begin in the center of the butcher paper, spiraling out. Make two circles in this manner, one for the snowman's head, and one for his body.
4. Cut a tall black hat from the black construction paper. Cut two black eyes from the scraps.
5. Glue the hat, eyes, nose and mouth onto the snowman.
6. Hang him up and choose from the ideas listed below, or make up your own . . .
   Sing "Frosty the Snowman."
   Play "Snowman Melt" on page 56 of this book.
   Make up stories about the time your snowman:
   went ice fishing,
   met a sleeping bear,
   had a Snowman's Christmas,
   grew a tail.

YOU MAKE THE PAPER — CHRISTMAS CARDS

MATERIALS YOU WILL NEED
> one or more newspapers
>> torn into tiny shreds
>
> one or more cups of sawdust
> one plastic tub full of water
> spoon
> hand potato masher
> two 6x6" wooden frames
>> with a screen stapled in
>> the center
>
> paper towels
> newspapers
> two wooden blocks
> magic markers
> an iron
> an adult to supervise the ironing

WHAT TO DO
1. Drop the paper shreads and sawdust into the tub of water. Stir them with the potato masher.
2. Allow the mixture to soak overnight.
3. Scoop a thin layer of mixture into the wooden frame. Press out excess water with wooden blocks.
4. To prepare your paper for pressing, stack newspaper, then paper towel, then your wet paper, then another paper towel on top.
5. Press the iron firmly on the stack to help pack the new, wet paper and to iron out excess water.
6. Place the new card on fresh newspaper in the direct sunlight to dry. It may take a few days.
7. When dry, design the card before printing it. Make a rough copy. Then, using magic markers, print on it.
8. You did it!

VARIATION: Make the paper as directed above. When it is dry, carefully cut out the center to make a picture frame. Use the center as a small card.

ELF HAT

MATERIALS YOU WILL NEED
    needle and thread
    scissors
    one triangular piece of
      material
    rickrack scraps
    face paints or crayons
    an adult to supervise the sewing

WHAT TO DO
1. Thread and knot all needles prior to beginning this project. Also, discuss sewing safety with each elf.
2. Lay the triangle flat. Stitch the rickrack across the bottom of the hat.
3. With wrong sides together, measure the hat to fit the head. Stitch from the base up to the point of the hat.
4. Turn the hat right-side out and put it on!
5. Draw designs on the elf's cheeks, chin and nose with the face paints or crayons.
6. Have the children write a quick elf-skit and perform it in their costumes, or read "Busy Elves" on page 11 of this book.

EDIE'S DREIDLE

MATERIALS YOU WILL NEED
    one pencil
    one egg carton section
    felt tip pen

WHAT TO DO
1. Draw one of these four Hebrew letters on each side of the egg carton section.

    Nun: נ   Gimmel: ג   Heh: ה   Shin: ש

2. Push the pencil through the center of the bottom of the egg carton section to make a top.
3. With the black felt tip pen, draw one of these signs on each side of the dreidle.
4. Now you are ready to play the Dreidle Game. Turn to page 53 in this book to learn how to play.
5. The four letters stand for Nes Gadol Hayah Sham, or A Great Miracle Happened Here.

CRYSTAL SNOW SCENE

MATERIALS YOU WILL NEED
    one 9x12" sheet dark blue or black
      construction paper
    paint brush
    Epsom salt crystals
    hot, hot water
    one 1 qt. glass jar with lid
    crayons
    newspaper

WHAT TO DO

1. Pour a few Epsom salt crystals onto the newspaper to study. Explain that you will be mixing them with hot water, and will be watching for any changes that might occur in the structure of the crystal.
2. Fill the glass jar with hot, hot water.
3. Pour Epsom salt crystals into the water. Stir until they are dissolved. Continue adding Epsom salt crystals until they will no longer dissolve. The hotter the water, the more Epsom salts you will be able to add.
4. Discuss the changes that occurred in the crystals, then set aside to dry. *(You can store this mixture in-definitely.)*
5. Draw an outdoor snow scene, then color it in very solidly and heavily with crayons.
6. Set the picture on the newspaper.
7. Paint the Epsom salt solution over the entire drawing. Make sure every corner of the page is covered. While you are painting, notice again the crystals have turned to liquid.
8. Set the picture aside to dry flat. Slowly, the Epsom salt mixture will begin to whiten, looking like falling snow. In fact, each day the "snow" will become whiter and whiter. The children will delight in watching this phenomenon! This is an opportune time to notice that as the water evaporates, crystals form again.
9. Look through a magnifying glass. Count the sides on the crystals.

CHRISTMAS CARD HOLDER

MATERIALS YOU WILL NEED

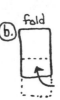

two 9x18" sheets white construction paper
one 9x18" sheet red construction paper
scissors
glue
pencil
blue, white, and red construction paper scraps for face

WHAT TO DO

1. Cut a cap from the red sheet of paper. *(illustration a)*
2. Glue the red cap to the top of one of the white sheets of paper.
3. Fold the bottom 1/3 of the white sheet up to make a pocket. *(illustration b)*
4. Glue the edges along the sides . . . not the top.
5. Fold the remaining sheet of white paper in half. Fringe the edges of both sides of the fold. Using the pencil, curl the fringes to make a curly beard. *(illustation d)*
6. Glue the beard to the top of the pocket.
7. From the scraps cut, fringe and curl two eyebrows. Glue them on. Cut and glue on two eyes, a nose, a mustache and a mouth. Add a curly top to the cap.
8. Hang in a convenient spot to display Christmas cards.

STAINED GLASS ELEGANCE

MATERIALS YOU WILL NEED
 a long string of black yarn
 1 foot waxed paper
 white glue
 magic markers

WHAT TO DO
1. Lay the waxed paper flat on a table top.
2. Make a circle with the black yarn, then continue to twist and curve the yarn in abstract designs inside the circle. Finish by leaving a tail of yarn at the top for hanging the piece.
3. Fill in the entire circle with white glue as high as the yarn.
4. Allow it to dry. It will dry clear.
5. Color the glue with magic markers.
6. Pull off the waxed paper and hang it in the window where it can catch the holiday sunbeams.

WRAPPING PAPER

MATERIALS YOU WILL NEED
    tissue paper
    thin tempera paint
    plastic straw or paint brush
    newspaper

WHAT TO DO
1. Lay the tissue paper on the newspaper.
2. Put one end of the straw in the paint. Before lifting it out of the liquid, place one finger over the opposite end of the straw. Lift the straw from the paint container to the tissue paper.
3. Slowly lift your finger, causing paint to drip on the tissue. Continue dripping paint onto the tissue to create interesting designs.
4. Be sure to warn the elves not to drink the paint through the straw.

VARIATION: Gift wrap your present in a box with any plain sheet of tissue paper. Using very thin, pastel tempera, paint a simple subject on the paper. It can be a bell, an angel, a tree, a reindeer, or a bird, for example. Use quick, long gentle strokes so the tissue does not become too watery and tear.

THE ELVES AND THE SNOWBEAR IN THE FOREST

MATERIALS YOU WILL NEED
a large playing area

HOW TO PLAY
1. Divide all the children into two teams, one team of elves and one team of trees. Select one child to be the Snowbear.
2. The trees should space themselves one arm's length from all of the neighboring trees.
3. When the game begins, the Snowbear will try to tag the elves as they run away through the trees.
4. Continue the chase until most or all of the elves have been caught.
5. Play the game again. This time the elves become trees and visa versa. Be sure to choose a new Snowbear.

SNOWBALL FIGHT ... OR RELAY

MATERIALS YOU WILL NEED
> one bucket for each team
> snowballs, an equal number for each team
> *(make them by wrinkling white paper napkins into small round balls)*
> two goal lines opposite each other

HOW TO PLAY
1. Divide the players into equal teams.
2. Hand each player a snowball(s).
3. One at a time, the players must run down to the bucket and deposit their snowballs, then return to the end of the line.
4. The first team finished is the winner.

VARIATION: Set up the buckets as a target. Have each member of the relay team take a turn tossing his snowball into the bucket. The first team to have all snowballs in the bucket is the winner ... and they can begin the SNOWBALL FIGHT!

THE ELVES' TREASURE HUNT

MATERIALS YOU WILL NEED
   a treasure
   a map to the spot where the treasure is hidden
   (x marks the spot where they can find it)

HOW TO PLAY
1. When all of the elves are gone, hide the treasure.
2. Draw a treasure map, send the elves in every direction in search of the hidden prize. Be sure to mark the spot with an x.
3. Give the map to the elves and let them discover on their own where the treasure is located.
4. The treasure can be buried inside or outside.
5. Once the elves have found the treasure, have them divide into small groups and draw treasure maps for others to follow. Exchange the maps after the treasures have been hidden.
6. What fun!

For Older Children

Can You Find The Treasure?
1. Walk through the door.
2. Take 3 paces forward.
3. Turn left.
4. Walk forward 15 steps.
5. Turn right.
6. Walk 10 steps forward.
7. Walk 3 steps backwards.
8. Crawl under the table to find your treasure.

For Younger Children

X

SANTA'S STORY STARTER

MATERIALS YOU WILL NEED
pencil and paper for older children
crayons and paper for younger children

WHAT TO DO
1. Read the poem,
"Where is Santa in the Spring?" on page 17 of this book. Use this poem as a story starter.
2. Ask younger children to illustrate what they think happens to Santa in the spring. Be sure to take dictation and write what they tell on their picture.
3. Ask older children to write what they think Santa does in the spring. Do not worry about grammar and punctuation in the first draft. Rather, encourage the children to capture their creative thoughts and record them. If you wish, you can attend to editing and revision after the rough draft has been shared.

SHIRA'S DREIDLE GAME

MATERIALS YOU WILL NEED
one dreidel *(see page 46 in this book)*
tokens *(pennies, buttons or nuts)*
pot

HOW TO PLAY
1. Each player takes some tokens.
2. Each player places one token in the pot.
3. Take turns spinning the dreidle.
When the dreidle stops on a Nun, **ℶ**
the player takes nothing.
When the dreidle stops on a Gimmel, **ℷ**
the player takes all tokens in the pot.
When the dreidel stops on a Heh, **ה**
the player takes half.
When the dreidle stops on the Shin, **ש**
the player must add one token to the pot.
After a player lands on a Gimmel, each player adds another token to the pot so the game can continue.

SNOWMAN MELT

MATERIALS YOU WILL NEED
    a large circle drawn on the floor
    appropriate music, such as
      "Frosty the Snowman"

HOW TO PLAY
1. Have all the children stand on the circle. Explain that they are snowmen as long as the music is playing. When the music stops, the sun will come and melt them away. They do not wish to melt. So they drop to the floor to hide from the sun. The last child down on the floor will be "melted."
2. Play the music while the snowmen skip around in the circle.
3. Stop the music and all of the snowmen must drop to the floor.
4. The last snowman to drop must sit on the side in a "puddle" to become your helper.

HAPPY-HAPPY HOLIDAYS

MATERIALS YOU WILL NEED
two goal lines

HOW TO PLAY
1. All children stand on one of the goal lines. The child that is IT stands in the center between the goals.
2. The child at one end of the line begins the game by calling "happy." Then the child next to him calls "happy," and so on down the line. The last person in line calls HOLIDAYS!
3. At that moment, all children drop hands and run for the other goal while Santa tries to tag the players.
4. Those players who have been tagged remain in the center to help Santa.
5. Continue play until most or all players have been caught.

VARIATION: **SANTA AND THE REINDEER**

HOW TO PLAY
1. All children stand on one goal line. Each child selects the name of one of Santa's reindeer for himself . . . Dasher, Dancer, Prancer, Vixen, Comet, Cupid, Donner, Blitzen, or Rudolph.
2. One child is Santa Claus and goes to the center to be IT.
3. When Santa calls the name of a reindeer, all the reindeer with that name must run to the opposite goal before being tagged by Santa. If tagged, the child goes to the center to help Santa tag other reindeer.
4. The last reindeer to be tagged is the new Santa.

TOYLAND

MATERIALS YOU WILL NEED
    a picture of a toy drawn on a piece of paper and
        folded in half for each child playing the game
    a basket to hold the papers

HOW TO PLAY
1. Have the children sit in a circle.
2. Begin by letting one child draw a paper from
   the basket. He pantomimes playing with the toy.
   The others try to guess what the toy is.
3. Work around the circle so all the children have
   a chance to act out one toy.

HOP IN SANTA'S SLEIGH!

MATERIALS YOU WILL NEED
    the pictures of toys used in the game above
    a circle drawn on floor

HOW TO PLAY
1. Have all children sit on the circle holding their
   toy. One child will be Santa Claus standing in
   front of the group.
2. Santa pretends he is driving his sleigh around
   the room picking up toys for his trip. As he calls
   the name of the toy a child is holding, that
   child hops aboard Santa's sleigh and follows
   Santa with his hand on Santa's shoulder.
3. Santa continues to collect "toys" until he calls,
   "Reindeer, up and away!" At that time, all the
   toys and Santa tumble out of the sleigh and
   back to the circle as fast as they can. *(You see,
   the reindeer climbed too steeply!)*
4. The last player to reach the circle is Santa
   Claus in the next game.

ONE GIFT FOR CHRISTMAS

MATERIALS YOU WILL NEED
one circle drawn on floor

HOW TO PLAY
1. Have all the children sit on the circle.
2. Ask the first child to name one gift he will give for Christmas. (It can even be a smile, the sunshine, a coupon for a walk around the block . . . anything.)
3. Ask the second child to name what the first child said, then add his gift for Christmas.
4. Continue around the circle. Each child must name all of the gifts he can recall before mentioning his gift.
5. You might wish to make a list of the gifts the children would like to give and send it home to the parents.

EXAMPLE:

CHILD I
I am giving a bear hug for Christmas.

CHILD II
I am giving a bear hug and a handshake for Christmas.

CHILD III
I am giving a bear hug and a handshake and a slide down a rainbow for Christmas.

CHILD IV
I am giving a bear hug, a handshake, a slide down the rainbow, and one wish granted.

OR . . . you can designate a topic, OR . . . let them tell about gifts they would truly like to give.

AN ORIGINAL CHRISTMAS PLAY

Have the children write their own Christmas play. Older children can work in groups, doing the writing themselves, while younger children can dictate to an adult. Set down a few ground rules before beginning, such as no violent or angry scenes. Make sure EVERY child gives input. Emphasize keeping the plot simple.

When the play has been transcribed, rewrite it with dialogue so all children have a role.

Assign parts and practice. Have the children design and paint their own sets and costumes. They can be as simple as a butcher paper backdrop and stick masks held in front of the face. Be SURE to invite parents and/or another class to attend a performance.

Oh, they'll be so *proud* of themselves!

M-E-R-R-Y C-H-R-I-S-T-M-A-S

MATERIALS YOU WILL NEED
one card with each letter of the words MERRY
  CHRISTMAS
circle
one bell

HOW TO PLAY
1. Have all of the children sit on the circle.
2. Pass out the letters around the circle.
3. When the bell rings, the children begin to pass the letters around the circle as fast as they can.
4. When the bell rings again, the passing stops.
5. Each child holding a letter when the bell rings must stand with the others to spell Merry Christmas in the correct order.
6. Each child must name his letter, then say one word which begins with that letter.
7. When all of the children have had a turn, they return to the circle and pass the letters again.

VARIATION: Older children can make up silly tongue twisters that begin with the letter they are holding.

Delicious
Elfen
Treats

HOOP — SWEETS

INGREDIENTS YOU WILL NEED
    one hoop
    ribbon and green boughs
    scissors
    candy, nuts, fruit, cupcakes, etc.
    clear plastic wrap

WHAT TO DO
1. Decorate the hoop with ribbons and boughs. Tie ribbons so that the hoop can be hung from the ceiling.
2. Wrap the treat you have chosen in the clear plastic wrap.
3. Tie each sweet treat with a ribbon and hang it from the hoop low enough for the children to reach.
4. Have the children take the magic scissors and cut down their treat . . .
    OR winners of games take a treat . . .
    OR have the children blow bubbles and when their bubble hits it, they may have that treat . . .
    OR distribute numbers to each child that correspond with a number on one of the treats.

CHRISTMAS TREE ORNAMENTS

INGREDIENTS YOU WILL NEED

1 c. table salt
2 c. flour
1 c. water
bowl and spoon
nail, fork, knife
white glue and glitter
paint and brushes
varnish and brush

rolling pin
cookie cutters
cookie sheet
string

WHAT TO DO

1. Pre-heat the oven to 325°.
2. Combine salt, flour and water in mixing bowl. Add just a little water at a time.
3. Knead the dough 7 to 10 minutes.
4. Roll out the dough to ¼" thickness. Cut into shapes with cookie cutters.
5. Using the nail, make a hole at the top to hang on the tree when the ornament is done.
6. Using the nail, fork or knife, draw final designs in the dough. Then bake at 325° for 30 minutes or until hard.
7. When cool, varnish to protect from moisture.
8. Decorate by drawing designs with white glue and glitter, or by painting. Set aside to dry.
9. Hang your homemade ornament on the Christmas tree.

CRANBERRY RED PUNCH

INGREDIENTS YOU WILL NEED
    2 qt. (8 c.) cranberry juice
    ¼ c. grenadine syrup
    2 qt. Club soda chilled
    punch bowl
    ladle
    ice cubes
    one cup of strawberries or cherries, optional

WHAT TO DO
1. Combine the chilled cranberry juice and grenadine in punch bowl.
2. Slowly add Club soda.
3. Add ice cubes. Garnish with strawberries and cherries.
4. This recipe serves about 32 elves.

OLD FASHIONED HOLIDAY POPCORN BALLS

INGREDIENTS YOU WILL NEED
  6-7 quarts popped corn
  2 c. molasses
  3-4 T. butter
  1 stick butter
  1 bowl for the popcorn
  2 baking sheets
  one 3 quart kettle
  hot pads
  spoons
  an adult to supervise cooking
  plastic bags or tin foil

WHAT TO DO
  1. Butter the baking sheets lightly.
  2. Pour the molasses into the kettle and bring to a slow boil. Stir constantly. Continue boiling until the molasses begins to thicken and is frothy, or full of air bubbles. Do not undercook leaving the molasses thin and runny.
  3. Butter your hands thoroughly. Many hands make light work!
  4. Pour the hot, thick molasses over the popcorn. Stir the popcorn into the molasses. Quickly mold the popcorn into round balls about the size of an apple.
  5. Place the popcorn balls on the baking sheet to cool.
  6. If there are more popcorn balls than munching elves, save them by wrapping them in plastic bags or tin foil.
  7. Tie a ribbon around one and leave it out for Santa!

ELVES' PEANUT CLUSTERS

INGREDIENTS YOU WILL NEED
- 1 package chocolate or vanilla pudding
- 1 c. sugar
- ½ c. evaporated milk
- 1 T. butter
- wooden spoon
- pot
- 1 c. peanuts
- teaspoon
- waxed paper

WHAT TO DO
1. Combine pudding, sugar, milk and butter in pan.
2. Bring to boil, stirring constantly.
3. Stir in peanuts until the mixture begins to thicken.
4. When the thickening begins, drop the elves' peanut clusters onto waxed paper using a teaspoon.
5. Do not store them where the elves will find them, or they might disappear!

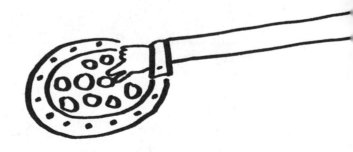

CHANUKAH COOKIES

INGREDIENTS YOU WILL NEED

2 c. flour
1 c. sugar
1/2 t. salt
2 t. baking powder
1 egg   Nun: נ
1/3 c. butter
1/4 c. milk
1 t. vanilla   Gimmel: ג
butter, oil or shortening
large bowl
measuring cup   Heh: ה
measuring spoon
beater   Shin: ש
sifter
bread board
rolling pin
dull knife for cutting
cookie sheet

WHAT TO DO

1. Cream butter and sugar in a large bowl.
2. In another bowl, beat the egg and add the milk and flavoring.
3. Stir both mixtures into a large bowl.
4. Sift together the flour, salt, and baking powder.
5. Add these ingredients into the large mixture and stir well.
6. Place the dough into the refrigerator for one hour.
7. Dust a bread board and rolling pin with flour.
8. Roll out the cool dough about ¼ of an inch thick.
9. Cut into the shape of the four dreidle letters.
10. Place on greased cookie sheet.
11. Bake in oven for 12 minutes at 350°.

LATKES *(Potato Pancakes)*

INGREDIENTS YOU WILL NEED
  3-4 medium potatoes, peeled and grated
  1 T. grated onion
  2 T. flour
  2 large eggs, well beaten
  ½ t. salt
  oil for frying
  skillet
  spoon and spatula
  paper towels

WHAT TO DO
  1. Mix flour with the grated potato and add well beaten eggs, grated onion, and salt. The smooth batter should drop heavily from the spoon. Add another egg if the mixture seems too dry or stiff.
  2. Heat the oil in a heavy frying pan and drop in spoonfuls, making pancakes about 3 inches in diameter. Fry over medium heat until brown on the underside. Turn and brown the other side.
  3. Lift out and drain on paper towels. The pancakes should be puffed and crispy.
  4. Serve hot with applesauce or sour cream.
  5. It is believed that *latkes* were prepared by the Jews to feed their hungry armies while they were doing battle with the Syrians. They are fried in oil to commemorate the oil of the *menorah*.

FRENCH CARAMEL CANDY

INGREDIENTS YOU WILL NEED
4 c. sugar
2½ c. white corn syrup
3 pints whipping cream (or real cream)
1 t. vanilla
1 deep kettle and wooden spoon
candy thermometer
walnuts
an adult to supervise cooking
one well greased 10½x15x1" cake pan

WHAT TO DO
1. Put sugar, corn syrup and ½ cup whipping cream into kettle. Bring to slow boil, stirring constantly.
2. Add another ½ cup whipping cream. Slowly boil. Continue until all whipped cream is blended. Continue to stir.
3. Cook at a slow boil until the temperature reaches 236°F, or Soft Ball stage on candy thermometer. It may take 1-2 hours. Stir frequently.
4. Stir in vanilla and walnuts while ingredients cook.
5. Pour into a well greased cake pan, and let stand to cool.
6. Even though this takes awhile, the elves think it is delicious.

Your Notes

CREDITS
EDUCATIONAL CO-OPERATIVE SCHOOL
REDDING, CALIFORNIA

KTAV COOKIE CUTTER COOK BOOK,
Aunt Fanny,
KTAV Publishing House, New York.

Mom, Paul Williams, Linda Jones, Susan Lynch, Florence and John Higgins, Edie Hughes, Gail Nall, Mary Burns, Joyce Huber, Peter Hartman, Maryjo Cordano-Callahan, Jacque Grubbs, Carol Hooper, Mary Springhorn, Louise Watson, Jan Clipper, Kathy Rich, Lil Daly and Melvin Phelps...

to all of you, please
accept my heartfelt thanks
for your wonderful ideas
and contributions.

Especially to my husband and children . . .
thank you for your patience and support
during the writing of this book.